By Rodney Jones

THE STORY THEY TOLD US OF LIGHT
THE UNBORN

The Unborn

The Unborn

POEMS BY Rodney Jones

The Atlantic Monthly Press
BOSTON / NEW YORK

FIRST EDITION

Copyright acknowledgments appear on page 79.

LIBRARY OF CONGRESS CATALOGING IN PUBLICATION DATA

Jones, Rodney, 1950–
  The unborn.

  I. Title.
PS3560.05263U5 1985   811'.54   84-71904
ISBN 0-87113-004-1
ISBN 0-87113-005-X (pbk.)

MV
Published simultaneously in Canada

PRINTED IN THE UNITED STATES OF AMERICA

For Gloria

Contents

ONE

Remembering Fire   3
Baby Angels   4
I Find Joy in the Cemetery Trees   6
A History of Speech   8
The Neckties   10
Friends of the Poor   12
Responsibilities   14
A Hill of Chestnuts   15

TWO

Sweep   19
The Safety Lecture   21
For Those Who Miss the Important Parts   23
Curiosity   25
Dirt   27
The Laundromat at the Bay Station   28
Thoreau   31
Edisonesque   32
Meditation on Birney Mountain   34

Some Futures   36
This Is Garvey's Delusion   38

THREE

The Mosquito   40
For the Eating of Swine   42
The First Birth   44
The Man Who Thinks of Stallions   46
Fledglings   47
Dry Socket   48
A Distant Weather   50
The Magic Cloak   52

FOUR

Imagination   57
Unpainted Houses   60
Two Girls at the Hartselle, Alabama,
    Municipal Swimming Pool   62
Alma   63
Recurrence of Acrophobia at an
    Abandoned Quarry   65
After the Maquilisuat Tree   67
Simulated Woodgrain Vinyl   70
Decadence   72

Acknowledgments   79

One

REMEMBERING FIRE

ALMOST as though the eggs run and leap back into their shells
And the shells seal behind them, and the willows call back their
    driftwood,
And the oceans move predictably into deltas, into the hidden
    oubliettes in the sides of mountains,

And all the emptied bottles are filled, and, flake by flake, the
    snow rises out of the coal piles,
And the mothers cry out terribly as the children enter their
    bodies,
And the freeway to Birmingham is peeled off the scar tissue of
    fields,

The way it occurs to me, the last thing first, never as in life,
The unexpected rush, but this time I stand on the cold hill and
    watch
Fire ripen from the seedbed of ashes, from the maze of
    tortured glass,

Molten nails and hinges, the flames lift each plank into place
And the walls resume their high standing, the many walls, and
    the rafters
Float upward, the ceiling and roof, smoke ribbons into the wet
    cushions,

And my father hurries back through the front door with the
    box
Of important papers, carrying as much as he can save,
All of his deeds and policies, the clock, the few pieces of silver;

He places me in the shape of my own body in the feather
    mattress
And I go down into the soft wings, the mute and impalpable
    country
Of sleep, holding all of this back, drifting toward the unborn.

BABY ANGELS

THIS one from the iron lung,
this one from the tornado,
this one was never born:
I look at the Christian names
of the children on the tombstones
in the cemetery at Buena Vista,
sweet meadow rolling
to sheep, green lawns, and corn.
You go there if nothing
else is happening in your life.
You go there if you own a plot
to see how the grounds hold up.
When I see the baby angels,
why do I think of vaccination day,
that long uneasy line, and always
the girl with thick glasses
crying on her fat brother's arm.
Part Cupid because they are intentional,
part Bacchus because they are frivolous,
the baby angels have trained
the cotton-mouthed mad dogs.
They own barrels of rusty nails,
rectangular country ponds
and their clouds of dark gnats.
And clearly, these children are here
for a reason. Some could not keep
their mouths shut. Their tongues
entered the infectious pencil grooves,

lapping up the beautiful names
of diseases. This one fell from a mule.
This one did not wear her galoshes.
All, on occasion, ignored the warnings
so the baby angels are all theirs now.
Fat with a grief that is distant
as they are faded, wings
spread for a wind strong enough
to lift them, they blurt out
a little water into the marble cups
of their hands and stare
with hard eyes over the pointless view.

I FIND JOY IN THE CEMETERY TREES

I FIND joy in the cemetery trees.
Their roots are in our hearts.
In their leaves the soul
of another century is in ascension.
I hear the rustling of their branches
and watch the exhausted laborers
from the Burgreen Construction Company
sit down in the shade,
unwrapping their cheese and bologna
and popping open their thermoses.
Apparently, they too are enamored
of the hickory and willow
at the edge of our cemetery,
the steadfast and lithe trunks
which contain so much of the dead.
While summer is too much with us,
they are stretching twine, building a wall,
as though this could be contained.
As they mix their mortar, as
they gossip about fistfights and big breasts,
probably they do not think
of our grandmothers who are pierced,
and probably they do not want
to hear about Thomas Hardy,
who, if I remember, has been dead
longer than they have been alive,
and who gave to the leaves of one yew
the names of his own dead. Anyway

the only spirits I can call in this place
are the stench of a possum
suppurating in secret weeds
and the flies, who are marvelous
because their appetite is our revulsion.
Let the laborers go on. Right now
I wish I could admire the trees simply
for their architecture. All winter
the dying have set their tables
and now they are almost as black
as the profound waters off Guam.
A few minutes ago, when they started
in a slight breeze off the lake,
the many patient and hopeless sails,
I could see in those motions
a little of the world that owns me —
and that I cannot understand —
rise in its indifferent passion.

A HISTORY OF SPEECH

THAT night my sophomore date wanted kisses.
I talked instead of the torn ligaments
in my ankle, crutches and Ace bandages,
parading like any arthritic
the exotic paraphernalia of my suffering
and, that failing, went farther, bobbing
in the thesaurus of pain: the iron lung,
the burn, torture with water and bamboo.
She twisted a frosted curl around one finger.
It was then she touched the skin along my neck.
It was then I noticed for the first time
the strange wing beating in my mouth
and kissed her in a kind of flight
that plummeted and clutched for branches.

Ah, but Tahiti of a thousand Tahitis!
Among the suckling cars of the drive-in,
trays of pomegranates, lingerie of surf.
Days I hurled papers onto the porches of invalids.
June nights I only had to open my mouth,
out came a flock of multicolored birds,
birds of all denominations and nationalities,
birds of nostalgia, the golden birds of Yeats,
birds trained in the reconnaissance of exclusive buttons.
Before I knew it I was twenty-two.
I was whispering into the ear of Mary,
the mother of Jesus. I was dreaming

in two languages I did not understand.
I was sitting in the bar of the Cotton Lounge,

railing against George Wallace, when the fist
rang in my stomach and I looked up
to a truckdriver shouting down at me,
"Talk too much!" Talk too much into greasy
footprint, linoleum stinking of beer,
the thigh of that woman rising to leave.
Talk too much and understand I'm not to blame
for this insignificance, this inflation
in the currency of language. Listen:
whenever I hurt, the words turned their heads;
whenever I loved too much, they croaked and hopped away.
At my luckiest, I'm only saying the grace
the hungry endure because they're polite.
Learning speech, Demosthenes put pebbles in his mouth,
but my voice is haunted by softer things.

THE NECKTIES

LET me hang around the driftwood long enough and I forget
        what it means to wear shirts and long pants,
to wait in line in the back of the department store while the
        alterations are being done.
I forget the pleats, the pressed creases, and the lapels of jackets,
the French cuffs hiding their ashes, their laundered balls of
        paper like spitwads from elementary school.
Let me sit down each morning at Sonny's, eating my poached
        eggs and bacon with the fishermen
whose faces have taken cancer from the sun, whose arms are
        stenciled with the names
of girls they met far from here, the strange anchors lifted from
        other seas.

After the first week the whiteness leaves, and the pale wishes of
        our city.
I walk all day through the bevies of sunbathers, and, because
        I'm old enough,
not every oiled thigh is leading up to a rendezvous out there in
        the dunes where the sea thistles itch
and misplaced spectacles burrow down among the roots of
        sawgrass.
By the third week I avoid company and don't wash except in
        seawater.
I welcome the old onion of my animal struggling up from the
        armpits.

I think I am becoming that ocean, defenseless as far as I am
 unbounded,
my shores polluted, my laughter coming in waves, my tears
 rising with my gall.

The charm is to approach nakedness, the hand almost touching
 the wild bird, almost the song
coming apart in the hand — but our smallest fashion is like the
 neon sign under the palm branch,
advertising our dominion and holy separateness, and I must
 remember again my father's neckties
slipping through my hands in the cool closet, the synthetic and
 silk tentacles
of a respectability he married in his mind to clean nails and
 chandeliers.
Tying them scrupulously, the way a winter fisherman ties the
 perfect fly, he went out to his job
with his words cramped and his breath hobbled to the logos of
 his good life.

In memory I hoard each tie, fashioning the serpent and the
 hangman's noose, as I have lingered
over the pebbles of his alligator shoes and watched his suits
 above me fill with years of duplicate Sundays.
His secret ritual, to keep the world always at his throat, I have
 buried among the susurrations of his disapproval.
Naked tonight, I swim halfway to my father, the yokes of his
 dead gods fallen around me.
In my exhaustion I lie in the welts of moonlight on the sand,
 relying this time on the nose,
the forgotten sense of the twentieth century, to show me again
 the rancor and the lost essences,
to separate the odor of sex from the odor of death in the odor
 of the sea.

FRIENDS OF THE POOR

In January when the pipes froze
and rotting snow cluttered the ditches,
the Emmanuel Baptist Church
sent to my front door
(in immaculate appointments)
three cheerleaders for the soul.
Worse men have been called
under better conditions,
but I'd already been saved
twice earlier that week
by black angels with jumper cables.
I mean I'd been nursing a bone
grudge against the cold,
budgeting what grace I could muster,
and here were missionaries,
dressed for a mission, showing
the tract and good teeth of dogma.
Outside I showed them
freezing rain on each of the seven
steps to eternal riches.
Later, when George dropped in, holding
one knee because he'd fallen,
I told him about this.
He looked leached and threadbare,
said he'd been balling
Teresa the better part of the night.
Sometimes my friend is the good music
that feels its way

along a barbwire of static.
It's an old story, the used voice
the poor can afford late at night
when all that comes through
are the blues
and this small brilliance,
summoning words,
that begins in the heart
as applause.

RESPONSIBILITIES

ALL day, with ax and bucksaw, my grandfather
goes against oaks, poplars, and hickories,
building toward winter the heat his heart will not

coax now into the blunt tips of his fingers,
though the chainsaw, unboxed in the closet,
would be smarter to use, if he must do this at all,

as he has done every autumn of this century,
reading the growth rings in each log,
the blurred pages in the atlas of rain.

He swings against frost and the surgeon's wishes.
He feels the shell constrict around him.
He rocks each bone in its raggedy hammock.

And what can my mother do
now when he talks of marrying? His angel
calls daily from the projects. Almost his age,

she sits transfixed by soap operas.
In her, my mother sees
the laundry double, the bleached, obligatory

underthings pied with sulphurous flowers.
Say no to love? He gilds it yes —
hard-of-hearing, hearing

what he wants to hear. So she twists
in the talon of the second mothering.
These afternoons on the porch

he stacks his logs higher and higher
toward the spider
brooding over the calculus of her web.

A HILL OF CHESTNUTS

ALL over the woods seedlings still sprout
from the useless crotches of chestnuts,
shoot green and straight, toss
and are blighted, and die into stiffness:

dead wood all over, blackening,
here and there a beech blasted by lightning,
the ache one feels like music
where fire scored the trunk,

but not tragic like the extinct chestnut,
the worm-mitered and cottony fallen.
And it is not like the shaky marriage
of memory and hope, which we see

and do not see, in the root-fist
gripping the boulder, where the oak,
that overcomer, rises improbably
from the mineral absurdity of stone

and the heart is astonished, the air
singed by so many green torches.
Finally, to burn like that! Once
all I had left to love was color:

I relished poverty like a mouth, cheap
salads in the kitchen of a friend
who every evening got less friendly.
One time — I was a kid — a poor man,

a friend of my father's, had died.
We dug the grave. I was down there

in the hole, beating at the clay
with a pick, laughing, when the bottom

gave: then I sank through feathery
manacles that felt like chestnut
humus, hands of the dead, all
that sticky wing-beating at my ankle.

I came up quick. "Go back down,"
my father said, and I went softly,
tapping at the door of the earth.
Over my head he found the simple stone

coiled by privet, the name and date.
Sometimes I'll feel a hand
come up through the pavement.
Then doom recedes from me, like a hairline,

but when I see chestnuts going
down into their hills forever,
some standing fierce as missiles,
holding a pitiful green out from the rot,

I want to walk out into the streets
with all the foolish self-righteous,
carrying the signs of redemption,
maybe not to shout, only to move

cautiously as though in silence,
which guards terrible secrets.
And I think of pie safes and cupboards,
the yellow and black-grained wood of chestnuts.

Two

SWEEP

THE two Garnett brothers who run the Shell station here,
who are working separately just now,
one hunched under the rear axle of Skippy Smith's Peterbilt
        tractor,
the other humming as he loosens the clamps
to replace my ruptured heater hoses,
have aged twenty years since I saw them last
and want only to talk of high school
and who has died from each class.
Seamless gray sky, horns from the four-lane,
the lot's oil slicks rainbowing and dimpling with rain.
I have been home for three days, listening to an obituary.
The names of relatives met once,
of men from the plant where he works,
click like distant locks on my father's lips.
I know that it is death that obsesses him
more than football or weather
and that cancer is far too prevalent
in this green valley of herbicides and chemical factories.
Now Mike, the younger brother,
lifts from my engine compartment
a cluster of ruined hoses,
twisted and curled together like a nest of blacksnakes,

and whistles as he forages in the rack
for more. Slowly, the way things work down here,
while I wait and the rain plinks on the rims of overturned
        tires,
he and my father trade the names of the dead:
Bill Farrell for Albert Dotson,
Myles Hammond, the quick tackle of our football team,
for Don Appleton, the slow, redheaded one.
By the time the rack is exhausted
I'm thinking if I lived here all year I'd buy American,
I'd drive a truck, and I'm thinking
of football and my father's and Mike's words
staking out an absence I know I won't reclaim.
Because I don't get home much anymore,
I notice the smallest scintilla of change,
every burnt-out trailer and newly paved road,
and the larger, slower change
that is exponential,
that strangeness, like the unanticipated face
of my aunt, shrunken and perversely stylish
under the turban she wore after chemotherapy.
But mostly it's the wait, one wait after another,
and I'm dropping back deep in the secondary
under the chill and pipe smoke of a canceled October
while the sweep rolls toward me from the line of scrimmage,
and Myles Hammond, who will think too slowly
and turn his air-force jet into the Arizona desert,
and Don Appleton, who will drive out on a country road
for a shotgun in his mouth, are cut down,
and I'm shifting on the balls of my feet,
bobbing and saving one nearly hopeless feint,
one last plunge for the blockers
and the ballcarrier who follows the sweep,
and it comes, and comes on.

THE SAFETY LECTURE

A DAY's production, seventy miles of tubes —
but tubes hide in the lungs of air conditioners,
in the secret glands of distilleries,
and whoever keeps his cool
or sips his bourbon,
deftly flicking ashes with a free hand,
will not think how a thumb
catches in the toothed wheel.
Rolled out flat, a hand is a hamburger
occasioning the safety lecture.
Five-fingered, like a star, it glitters
in the nightmare where it is found,
washed up on the beach in Wilmington,
in Grand Forks, locked in the trunk
of a car or pointing to the
foundry, the press, the extruding
table, the pointer, and the saw
in the safety lecture. No wound
is impersonal, they say to factory hands
in Ensley, where the stubs of chimneys
are bleeding into the air
like hooked trout into mountain streams.
Loss of an eye that sees mounds
of lemons, lichen, and intimate gnats
might be prevented if you would wear
your safety glasses, but that eye
is not the problem, they say
in the safety lecture. Problems
with downtime are problems with personnel

that might be corrected somehow,
as in Huxley's *Island,* where there are birds
all over the island, saying
pay attention, pay attention
here and now, here and now
at the margins of the safety lecture.
And at the margins of the machines
the foreman stalks his shark circle like a pit boss
casing a casino for luck.
In the factory tropics he lets his gaze drift
across hands that pull the same lever
again and again, each man longing
for the jackpot to slide down his chute:
a month in the Grand Caymans,
woman with black hair
leading him across the sands
through the palmettos and coco palms
down to the dangerous calumny of the sea.

FOR THOSE WHO MISS
THE IMPORTANT PARTS

THE year Truman fired MacArthur
my uncle returned
from the hospital at Decatur,
his left hand torn
from the wrist, milled
into a ghostly bin
of Martha White Self-Rising Flour.
While Oscar Garrett ranted,
"We ought to get the bastards
before they get the bomb,"
and his wife, Mildred, went
to the kitchen for more custard,
the blue stump slipped out
of its flannel sleeve,
puffy and knuckled
like the head of a cottonmouth.
I didn't know pain had a phantom,
a thorn, like frostbite,
that ran long and clean
to the bone of emptiness.
I don't know yet whether
the coal stove or shame
flushed my father's face
with roses. While important
history went on elsewhere,
while the tough March wind
punched the window frames

and kicked at the glass bulb
in the heel of the thermometer,
my father and uncle were
almost as old as I am now.
Now I wish I were Li Po
with a Yangtze and plum blossom
to praise, with a poem
hard as jade to lay
on the threshold of annihilation.
If MacArthur had marched into China,
the map would still be yellow,
or I would not remember
so much my uncle's good hand
cold on my brow, and how my eyes
fell then, out of shyness,
running along the floorboards,
passing over his brown shoes,
over the knots
with their difficult wings.

CURIOSITY

WHAT does a tomato know?
Dangling between the nineteenth and twentieth centuries
on a vine with weak knees,
it has avoided the hoe and hailstone
and carries secretly
a balm for the hangover, a pungent sauce
to embellish the full
and indolent body of linguine.

I sit on the pot and read James Joyce
and then a little Robinson Jeffers
before thinking of my great-grandfather,
Andrew Jackson Jones,
who read almost nothing
and believed people could die
of tomatoes.

Imagine coming out of a black locust grove
on a cool late summer morning
in Alabama ninety years ago
to pick the first tomato in that part of the world.
My great-grandfather must have meditated
a long time on the unprecedented taste
of that tomato. I think
he believed poison was an indescribably smooth skin
covering a soft heart. I think he did not know
whether to add sugar or salt
to tame the wild taste of that tomato.

What did my great-grandfather know?
Turning the earth of the nineteenth century

over into the twentieth,
he had already followed the streaked hams of horses
for thirty years
and had a right to his distrust and ignorance.

What do any of us know
of the infinite possibilities
of tomatoes?

DIRT

I AM not a saint. All
that I am coming to
is crusting under my nails.
I am dragging my dull hoe
through the peppercorns
and letting the malathion snow
from the twin clouds
of my rubber gloves.
Here I am, the marshal
come to rescue the schoolgirls!
Here I am, the fat messiah
of the family! My aphids
twitch, of abstraction
and consequence bereft. They
linger in the narcotic hair
of the okra like glue,
their love's labor multiplied.
But I am merely exhausted
and hot. Sweat
clings to my brow
like thorns, my face
is flawed with the maps
of continents I shall never see.
My cleanliness is next to sleep.
When I look into the mirror,
when I lower my head
into the cool basin,
it is mercy I think of.
I keep trying
to grab some purity
in the water pouring over my hands.

THE LAUNDROMAT AT THE BAY STATION

WHEN the separation hit me with its tonnage, self-soiling,
      guilt,
I used to go there, having no other choice, void of the
      machinery of renewal,
carrying a pillowcase of spoiled shirts slung over one shoulder,
      bundling
in a mildewed towel my knot of blue jeans, underwear, and
      dirty sheets, my legacy, my impossible dowry.
I think I had never been so lonely, and the girl, Shirley, acned,
leafing through a magazine of teenage stars, who gave change
in the Kwik-Mart next door when the change machines were
      broken, seemed either
contemptuous or flirtatious, hot-tempered, feigning an
      incredible wound.
I could hear the cycles kick on and off and, underneath, the
      continuous roar
of water surging up from the valves, and I remember, once I
      was inside,
how the dark outside would grow rigid, as though I had
      entered,
after all of Oklahoma, the green and narcotic light of a
      truckstop restroom —
the rubber dispensers on the wall, the mirrors that magnify the
      pores.
Most of the customers I don't remember, but I can't forget
the divorcées in tight black stretch pants, cautiously sorting
      their lace panties, talking too loud
and pulling their stringy, cotton-headed kids out of the
      garbage pails,

whole families, sallow and almost retarded, and improbable
       younger girls,
big blondes who seemed to leap out of the rain, their hair
       frosted and piled high on their heads,
their spike heels clicking on the linoleum tiles gummy with diet
       soda.

It hurts me, that separateness, and how I lived then, mostly in
       one room, my bed a delirium of books,
everything else on the floor — dishes, fishing tackle, wadded
       sheets of typing paper,
the bedsprings leaning against one wall wired to a black and
       white tv.
Through the wall I heard arguments, then thuds, something
       heavy, maybe chairs
being thrown, doors slamming, then the bass throbbing over
       the weeping.
That year filth was the ledger I kept, marking each shirt, each
       towel.
Now that I'm happy, I need illness or blows before the
       Laundromat rises from the ashes
of my fever and confusion, and I can tell my wife how I
       looked at this one's thighs
or that one's enormous and floppy breasts as she knelt to take
       her sad underthings
from the dryer; how much I wanted their vulnerability, their
       poverty and hatred still to be there
once I was happier; and how much I wanted happiness then,
       even there,
smelling the faint and artificial odors of lemon blossoms,
       searching the wire baskets
for the mates to mismatched socks, the crude angels of
       embarrassment.

Almost a year and a half of my life has been blocked out,
       washed clean, the disease
of the self quarantined, checked there, and I don't want to
       think

about the laundry spinning in each washer, the dryers stationed
    like robots,
and the rejected people waiting, as though for a simple
    resurrection.
I don't want a new life spun clean of its dirt and chaos. The
    day my wife's mother,
my wife, and I came down the mountain from Santa Tecla to
    La Libertad,
El Salvador, I had been waiting for the river that runs
    through that place, even with the war there,
the way the women, some with their blouses off, were sitting
    on the rocks
with baskets of laundry to be knuckled and scrubbed, the
    children
splashing in and out of the shallow green pools left in the dry
    season,
and stretched beside them the shirts for labor and the shirts for
    dancing, the shirts for God
and the shirts for dying, all were whitening, were slowly
    drying around their stains,
and the laughter and the Spanish came up to me through the
    almond trees,
purely and without reason, rising on the small wind like birds.

THOREAU

Iᴛ is when I work on the old Volvo,
lying on my back among the sockets,
wrenches, nuts, and bolts,
with the asphalt grinding the skin
over my shoulderblades, and with the cold grease
dripping onto my eyeglasses,
that I think of Thoreau
on his morning walks around the pond,
dreaming of self-sufficiency.
I think of the odometer that shows
eight circuits of the planet.
I drop the transmission and loosen
the bolts around the bellhousing.
I take it in both hands, jerk,
and it pops like a sliced melon.
Carefully, so I won't damage
the diaphragm, I remove the clutch
and place it on a clean cloth
beside the jackstand. I look
at the illustrations in the manual
and I think of the lists that Thoreau made.
By the time I get to the flywheel,
grease is clotted in my hair,
my knuckles are raw and bleeding
against the crankcase, and I am thinking
of civil disobedience. I am looking
up into the dark heaven of machinery,
the constellations of flaking gaskets,
and I am thinking of Thoreau's dry cow,
of his cornstalks splintered by hail.

EDISONESQUE

WHATEVER the lights do, the possum is still with us
        these first nights of February,
foraging among the garbage pails of the rest stop
then waddling down to the interstate
        in the stillness, bending
to sniff the strange yellow paint of the center line.

Glum spelunker, she carries her own cavern
under signs that mark cities and distances.

In the sudden headbeams, what can she do
        but freeze,
who has taken so much of the dark into her swampy heart,
she would faint against every danger?

One winter night in Florida
I swayed beneath the world's largest Christmas tree,
dazzled by the 70,000 lights
winking off and on outside the offices of the *National Enquirer*.

To the possum, a match flaring behind a distant window
        must be that scandalous.
She tastes the good grimace of last salt
and takes the wheel into her papery shoulder.

Her last thought, though, is no more perceptible to me
than the shadow of a hummingbird wing
flickering through the shadow of a tree.

That night in Florida, after Lantana's phantasmagoric tree,
        we cruised Palm Beach,
gawking at the dream mansions of Kennedys and
        Steinbrenners —

the jewelers, banks, bistros, boutiques,
and flea-free terriers of Worth Avenue.

How long will the possum lie there
before I remember again?
The soul of a possum is an empty wallet
tossed into a trash bin by thieves.

What matters are these good lights shining in our faces.
        All winter
in the luminous hives of chickens there are no
        predators, and the ovaries
go on ripening, springing their white rivers of eggs.

MEDITATION ON BIRNEY MOUNTAIN

TODAY I come out of the thicket tired, without words,
my thighs dragging from the long artery of the watershed,

the yellow brick-clay of Alabama gumming my bootsoles,
and, while the heart slows, think of the kit fox

slowing, gathering his haunches in the last resolution
before the kill, or how, below me in the valley,

the Fairview Church of God, the punctual hedgerows
hiding their rabbits, and the dozen or so houses

of relatives seem to float in the slanting snow
like an Alpine village trapped inside a paperweight.

After the war my father came up here with his crew
of laborers from Powell's Chapel. They hacked

and gutted. They cut a brown swath wide as a gridiron
across five blue mountains for the TVA right-of-way.

Now his labor is silent. Only the cables hum
with light that rinses the screens of televisions

with the red juice of Apples that have our numbers
coded beside our names in the Crockett National Bank.

And farther on, where humus feathers the ridgeline,
it is the woodpecker, his appetite the deepest percussion.

It is the pulse of an old word, its connotations lost,
only the worm of meaning scarring the hollow trunk.

I was seven when my grandfather first brought me here
to the big sinkhole dished out beneath the southern peak,

where he let a stone drop in 1896 and heard the *ping*
and *thit* on and on, against the bottomless pitch

of the abyss, heard, past creekwater and seepage,
the dim beast snicker from the quick of the mountain.

Now rubbish stoppers the sinkhole: bedsprings
        where we loved,
heaped beer cans turned the color of fallen leaves.

It seems smaller now, and frivolous, like the ironies
of adolescence, like the upsurging of the green testicles.

Today I climb higher to look for fossils in a boulder
that gives its age stubbornly: first, a cloudy gash

that is so much like one of those fluted scars
the propellers of pleasure boats carve into the backs

of sea manatees; and when I look closer still,
when I strip back the nibs of lichen, the nut-fleshed

ears of moss, I can make out the leaf-shape and filigreed
spines of the first letters in the language of limestone.

I can touch like braille my old fathers, the *graptolites,*
the years that harden toward me, looking at the bare

bush inside my palm, bowled over by the radiance,
the nostalgia for stars. Until I turn away

stumbling into saplings, tripping headlong into gullies,
I am thinking like a bucket falling down the well of heaven

and I come down the mountain above my mother's house
like Moses with strangely inscribed tablets.

SOME FUTURES

BECAUSE the hands blacken, because that tired mule,
       the heart, drags
feet as blue as plums, and because the future's word,
       disease, is exactly right,
the future is far and away too ornamental
       in these essays I must judge,
as in Kubrick's *2001: A Space Odyssey*
       when the ship approaches
for so long an immense obscurity, and then
       a terrifying brightness,
that world where everyone is clinically bald
       and breath comes sweet
with the touch of a hidden button in our sides.

In these essays written by the graduating seniors
       of Greene County High Schools
and the Greeneville City Schools
       we move through the starry air
in vehicles of pure longing, touching here
       and there the bare
essential terraces of the future, that scalding light,
       and the large green country
of Greene County often is shrunken but powerful,
       like a quasar, and still green
inside the windows of greenhouses
       where the gentle robots
go stuttering water over the veined leaves.

Almost, the word *green* does not exist here.
       In one essay, the skyline
of homely Greeneville (grown to six million)
       is described wonderfully

as a single-toothed jaw, but this is too familiar,
        and I already know
the bite of the Greeneville air suffused with sulphur,
        the air rose-pink with carcinogens,
and the smog bronzed like a baby shoe. I expect too
        the bomb, the unquestionably
brilliant but discombobulated speech of the mutant.

Here are the derelictions of hope, the polymers of fear.
        In COBOL and Fortran the future
sways abstractly, the wind chimes on my porch collide.
        In their glass pods the milky fetuses
of geniuses are ripening like dandelions.
        I am reluctant holding back
the green prize money of the Greene County Kiwanians,
        for there is talent here, there
is sex performed in perfect weightlessness,
        there are five cures for cancer,
and synthetic death dribbling from a rotted drain.
        Where are the stones
emeralded with moss lodged in the humus above Camp Creek?

Where are Blake, da Vinci, Isaiah, and Nostradamus?
        Sunday, driving past the decrepit
and falling houses of animals, I hear the radio
        evangelist promise the second coming.
Against my day of judgment, his sure voice burns
        like acetylene. He is happy
holding antiquated hell over the heads of his congregation,
        but in the newer visions,
the fresher hells of these essays, the future
        fills with lasers and particle beams.
The astronaut, gone since 2021, goes on circling
        Andromeda, his computer blinking
senselessly, no pushbutton to quell his eternal orbiting.

THIS IS GARVEY'S DELUSION

There are Russians in the telephone lines.
There are the invisible knives,
Fire sprouting everywhere just under the skin.
This is Garvey's delusion.
This is the chain mail of tin cans pinned to his coat,
And this is the Pontiac where he sleeps,
Armored against the electrical plague.
This is the welfare lady, acquainted with his case,
And this is his main dream,
The gas shell hissing and rolling
Through the bodies doubling over in his trench.
Sometimes in a quiet store
In Glade Springs, Virginia, with no warning
He will erupt, go off leaping,
Slapping himself like a kid in a drizzle of hornets.
Today he tells the storekeeper,
"It's hell. They won't let up on me."
He turns quickly, leaves with a rusty chiming.
They have perfected such listening devices:
All the ears in the pine cones,
All the antennae that every April
Put out the camouflage of new leaves.
It is better to speak only to those friends
You have known longer than memory
And then to choose your words
Cautiously, like a third wife.
There are Russians in the telephone lines.
There are the carbon whips, shaped like pain.

Three

THE MOSQUITO

I SEE the mosquito kneeling on the soft underside of my arm,
    kneeling
Like a fruitpicker, kneeling like an old woman
With the proboscis of her prayer buried in the idea of God,
And I know we shall not speak with the aliens
And that peace will not happen in my life,
    not unless
It is in the burnt oil spreading across the surfaces of ponds,
    in the dark
Egg rafts clotting and the wiggletails expiring like batteries.
Bring a little alcohol and a little balm
For these poppies planted by the Queen of Neptune.
In her photographs she is bearded and spurred, embellished
    five hundred times,
Her modular legs crouching, her insufferable head unlocking
To lower the razor-edge of its tubes, and she is there
    in the afternoon
When the wind gives up the spirit of cleanliness
And there rises from the sound the brackish oyster and squid
    smell of creation.
I lie down in the sleeping bag sodden with rain.
Nights with her, I am loved for myself, for the succulent
Flange of my upper lip, the twin bellies of my eyelids.
She adores the easy, the soft. She picks the tenderest blossoms
    of insomnia.
Mornings while the jackhammer rips the pavement outside my
    window,
While the sanitation workers bang the cans against the big
    truck and shout to each other over the motor,
I watch her strut like an udder with my blood,

Imagining the luminous pick descending into Trotsky's skull
        and the eleven days
I waited for the cold chill, nightmare, and nightsweat of
        malaria;
Imagining the mating call in the vibrations of her wings,
And imagining, in the simple knot of her ganglia,
How she thrills to my life, how she sings for the harvest.

FOR THE EATING OF SWINE

I HAVE learned sloppiness from an old sow
wallowing her ennui in the stinking lot,
a slow vessel filled with a thousand candles,
her whiskers matted with creek mud,
her body helpless to sweat the dull spirit.
I have wrestled the hindquarters of a young boar
while my father clipped each testicle
with a sharpened Barlow knife, returning him,
good fish, to his watery, changed life.
And I have learned pleasure from a gilt
as she lay on her back, offering her soft belly
like a dog, the loose bowel of her throat
opening to warble the consonants of her joy.
I have learned lassitude, pride, stubbornness,
and greed from my many neighbors, the pigs.
I have gone with low head and slanted blue eyes
through the filthy streets, wary of the blade,
my whole life, a toilet or kitchen,
the rotting rinds, the wreaths of flies.
For the chicken, the cow, forgetfulness. Mindlessness
blesses their meat. Only the pigs are holy,
the rings in their snouts, their fierce, motherly indignation,
and their need always to fill themselves.
I remember a photograph. A sheriff had demolished
a still, spilling a hundred gallons of moonshine.
Nine pigs passed out in the shade of a mulberry tree.
We know pigs will accommodate

demons, run into rivers, drowning of madness.
They will devour drunks who fall in their ways.
Like Christ, they will befriend their destroyers.
In the middle of winter I have cupped my hands
and held the large and pliable brain of a pig.
As the fires were heating the black kettles,
I have scrupulously placed my rifle between pigs' eyes
and with one clean shot loosened the slabs
of side-meat, the sausages that begin
with the last spasms of the trotters.
O dolphins of the barnyard, frolickers
in the gray and eternal muck, in all your parts
useful, because I have known you, this is the sage,
and salt, the sacrificial markers of pepper.
What pity should I feel, or gratitude, raising you
on my fork as all the dead shall be risen?

THE FIRST BIRTH

I HAD not been there before where the vagina opens,
the petals of liver, each vein a delicate bush,
and where something clutches its way into the light
like a mummy tearing and fumbling from his shroud.
The heifer was too small, too young in the hips,
short-bodied with outriggers distending her sides,
and back in the house, in the blue *Giants of Science*
still open on my bed, Ptolemy was hurtling toward Einstein.
Marconi was inventing the wireless without me.
Da Vinci was secretly etching the forbidden anatomy
of the Dark Ages. I was trying to remember
Galen, his pen drawing, his inscrutable genius,
not the milk in the refrigerator, sour with bitterweed.
It came, cream-capped and hay-flecked, in silver pails.
At nights we licked onions to sweeten the taste.
All my life I had been around cows named after friends
and fated for slaughterhouses. I wanted to bring
Mendel and Rutherford into that pasture,
and bulb-headed Hippocrates, who would know what to do.
The green branch nearby reeked of crawfish.
The heavy horseflies orbited. A compass, telescope,
and protractor darted behind my eyes. When the sac
broke, the water soaked one thigh. The heifer lowed.
Enrico Fermi, how much time it takes, the spotted legs,
the wet black head and white blaze. The shoulders
lodged. The heifer walked with the calf wedged
in her pelvis, the head swaying behind her like a cut blossom.
Did I ever go back to science, or eat a hamburger
without that paralysis, that hour of the stuck calf

and the unconscionable bawling that must have been a prayer?
Now that I know a little it helps, except for birth
or dying, those slow pains, like the rigorous observation
of Darwin. Anyway, I had to take the thing, any way
I could, as my hands kept slipping, wherever it was,
under the chin, by tendony, china-delicate knees,
my foot against the hindquarters of the muley heifer,
to bring into this world, black and enormous,
wobbling to his feet, the dumb bull, Copernicus.

THE MAN WHO THINKS OF STALLIONS

In his mind there are two of them
reared to combat, their hooves
thrown like waterfalls, so that they seem
to be trying, awkwardly, to embrace.
Their habits are old stories
but remembered faintly
in the gilded legends of childhood,
so close to the lamb, pig, and swan,
only their wildness places them now:
their great struggle and truth to heat.
And the mare who will mate with the winner
munches patiently her bruised clover.
Her tail is arched to admit entry,
her pied body, late summer sky
flecked with clouds, the rain coming on.
These last few weeks, homicides
in the papers, brother slaying brother
with ice pick or butcher knife,
the old rage comes back like frostbite:
I gun the engine of my Ford and run
two decent people off the road.
"She's not your girl!" I scream,
and a boulder lodges against my heart.
Later, of course, I will return,
my crime made fresh by local shame,
even though she's fat and he,
a bald and obtuse accountant, out of work
(I will have heard) these past eight months.
Then I will climb slowly out of my car
and throw a single rock
hard and symbolically
across the ditch to the pasture
where the last horse in Cullman County
will lift his ears and neigh
softly against the tyranny of fences.

FLEDGLINGS

REMEMBER the sparrows,
how if you touched the fledgling
too fat for wings,
the mother would not know her.
The song was not mournful.
Actually, most birds do not sing.
There is a kind of awkward rasping,
as of a fiddle the size of an aspirin
bowed by a twine of breath,
only then it made the shoebox a clock,
and you went to it
with iodine dropper and tweezers
that would never be beaks.
You placed the fledgling
on a branch outside the window,
watched, and no one came.
I think the house is the same
the daughter returns to
after lying most of the night
in the backseat of a car with a shipping clerk
at the end of summer.
Her blood glows just under the skin,
her blouse is tracked with touch,
and the father will not speak.
The mother stares into her needlepoint
as though the years
had been difficult,
or these threads were
straw and sticks, a brittle nest
coming apart now in her hands.

DRY SOCKET

I TURN over on my left side so the blood can drain off the bad
    nerve — 200-pound head,
hair festering like a turnip in its dark soil, nails curling and
    sharpening
for the feather and scale, for the rubbery jugular inside the
    throat of the lamb.
Time throbs now, like a star. I nurse a little numbness from
    the clove.
I let warmth swell from the itchy towel wadded under the
    mandible.
This is the pain of divination, Job's pain, condensed,
    luminescent.
From one o'clock to the earliest light tipping the thrushes
behind my blind neighbor's house to take up again their insane
    litany,
I am running my tongue along its enamel walls, polishing the
    leopard teeth and the cow teeth.
I am planing this altarpiece in my mouth. I am worshipping
    the thorny and the essential:
the mare with her foundered hoof; the field lark, her beak
    cracked by pellets.
It is something for the self, and something for the beast and
    godliness.
At its edge, the orange Valiant struggles off toward Reynolds
    Aluminum,
the paper thuds on the front porch. I can feel the sun pumping
    its clear oil into the apertures of lilies.
I am thinking, first, of the blond boy from first grade,

his teeth rotted black by Milky Ways, then of the carpenter
        who lives
two doors down the street, his good smile splintered by
        hammers and crowbars.
But, finally, it is my old shepherd, toothless and fierce, who
        comes back to me each morning,
toothmarked and torn, his pretty coat matted with the clay-
        colored blood.
Three-legged, half blind, he cannot give it up. His stupidity
        and vainglory keep him snapping
at the unrelenting night, even when it catches him and tosses
        him.
The clenched jaws shake at his withers and snout, yank, and he
        breaks with a popping
of cartilage, with a rifle-shot of bone, so he crawls back
        through the green cockleburs of exile.
When I find him, slumped against the tin of his toolshed, still
        as a feed bag, all the look gone
that sobered meanness, the look soaking to the center of his
        deep bruise, each morning
when I touch him, wading into the shallow breath at the end
        of his pride,
I place my hand in his mouth and take the tongue he will
        swallow.
I cradle the fruit of his toothless gum, delivered to the aurora
        of abscess, thinking, in pain's pure
meditation, how the tooth was named for wisdom because it
        came in so slowly.

A DISTANT WEATHER

Now my hunches go there like the rain:
impossible to confirm, but falling
from your hair onto your face,
gathering in puddles at your feet,
perhaps the same rain
that came here Tuesday or last week,
only now it has passed
through so many bodies,
emptied from so many glasses.
And just as the sky here
might have been there, my words
might once have been yours,
though none would clarify
your pain, silent and immovable,
when the weight of the night
settled on your brow
and you cried over the whistling kettle,
savoring the sweet vapor, the fabulous
dilemma of your wishes. I released you,
as one who shrugs and backs away
releases a significant doubt,
so there was no ceremony
of remorse, no sad afternoon,
only one day your address was gone,
your maiden name, the exact
fashion of your hair.
Neither can I be sure now

whether it was you or me,
or just which of us
these words are addressed to,
or whether that rain was this rain,
though obviously it was large enough.
Somewhere rivers must have flowed
into the streets, and always
in certain small places
someone gets drowned.

THE MAGIC CLOAK

THE stories I have read to her
come home in my daughter's words
when she talks to me
from fifteen hundred miles away
from a kingdom of dwarfs,
of zebras that float
under white zeppelins of language.
On the long line her tongue
blurs to foreign,
an ocean of static pounds
at the shore of her voice,
and all that comes through
is that she would be here
if she could wear the cloak
that Mickey the woodcutter
wore into the wizard's house.

For her, magic starts every car,
but I've grown tougher
from leaning into every illusion
that would have held me up.
I know that I'm here by luck,
she there by fate, that magic
might grow practical sides
impossible to accept or deny.
On Saturdays when the rates
are cheapest, that's when all
the sentimental fathers

throw their voices for miles
they can't afford to fly.
That's when all the words
are too old or too young,
my daughter and I, two birds
chattering in an immense
electrical flock. We
chippety doop, we figgledy jeep.
Wabbedy stack, we crow and peep.
The cows have had their puppies.
The mice are in our porridge.

Already I want us to talk
like two drunk and reunited friends.
I want to say that magic
comes true, more and more
at a distance, as the power
leaks from the elephant's battery,
and the doll's face, once
it is seen, was always hard.
The fish in the Holston River
fill with mercury,
the woodcutter runs out of walnuts.
Soon enough she will step down
from the plane, her coat
full of unaccustomed breasts.
I will tell her that to be happy
is to be cared for by someone
who cares as much for wisdom.
Because it's darker earlier here,
I will show her the talisman
of the first evening star.

Four

IMAGINATION

I AM just sitting, drinking bourbon, letting the heat spread
    across my skin like a bee-sting,
and waiting for my wife to return from a long-distance
    telephone call.
When I hear her a room away laughing and speaking Spanish
    to her mother,
I know that it was not meaning but her voice that I loved first,
and that nose, hand, eye, and tongue are more important than
    the philosophy of Locke or Kierkegaard.
I like to think of her voice rippling inside the talons of
    Mexican birds perched on the cables,
and then of the finches, bluebirds, mallards, and night herons
we saw last summer as we were canoeing the rapids of the
    Watauga River, backpaddling
frantically sometimes to detour around submerged rocks and
    deadfall,
or to keep our balance in the four-foot haystacks piling up in
    the gorges.
I know our lives were in that river, the clear interrupted flow,
    the threat always there
just under the surface, and the effort, among conflicting waves,
    to stay upright,
but I prefer the river simpler, bearing down from its great
    distance on the gulf,
moving through anonymous coves, oscillating among snail-
    dotted stones.
There would be long stretches of silence, and then suddenly a
    lone duck

would explode from the cattails at the edge of the current, one
      wing dragging theatrically,
squawking and carving a V in the water to distract danger
      from her nest.

What good is my life unless I save that bird, unless I let that
      river enter me now
as the sun enters through venetian blinds, laying down a
      keyboard of shadow and light,
and the slow composition of Beethoven breaks, one crystal at a
      time?
I tip my glass so the whiskey trickles and burns a little in my
      throat,
so the slivers of goat cheese and tart apples and the wheat
      crackers
my wife has laid out on the cutting board will come later
      as compensation,
like the afternoon, dissolving soreness, and the evocative
      melancholy of the piano.
We sat in the canoe, rocking in small waves, laughing at the
      absurd theater of that duck,
while her five ducklings bobbed free of the sanctuary of their
      cattails
and the leaf-shadows dappled the water with the vague rosettes
      of leopards.

Now I don't know any more than the ducks if imagination
      saves or betrays us,
as the mother dips her wing, cries purposefully, and is guided
      by uncertainty;
and the meaning, if it comes later, in one moment itself the
      confluence of many moments,
is survival through distraction, her art, the price of letting go.
Sometimes when my wife comes for me I'll be floating,
      dangling between sleep
and a wakefulness I can't arrange, so when her voice finally
      gets here

I'll want to tell her of Keats, how when death was so close to
      him he could taste
the bitterness of his own heart, he was freed by the song of a
      nightingale. Lately I've drunk too much.
There have been accusations and reprisals, and the images of
      the lives we've lived apart
have glanced off my wife and me like two keened blades losing
      their edges.
For Keats, his desire and fear were the same feather clinging to
      the cracked shell
of an egg so black and ominous its shadow laid the
      groundwork for numbness.
This afternoon, though, what I want is not death's image, and
      it is not the dream of desire,
but this simple delight in the commingling of four tastes, while
      the voice of my wife, the piano,
and the birds of last summer mark the vectors of a life divisible
      by water.

UNPAINTED HOUSES

THEY are all falling now, their dry skin peeling
to the November sun, their windows broken
so the snow may drift into rooms
where children colored the walls
with pencils and crayons,
but the children are gone now. Grown
into their own lives, crying
and warping a little from tenderness,
if they should think of home
it would be on a day like today, when the sky
takes its shape from the ruined branches of the dogwood
and everything turns the color of these unpainted houses,
everything naked,
unpresumptuous, and of an indeterminate gray.
These first cold days are like men, when the hormones
have released them, who will wait
on a streetcorner or sit at a plain table
with not so much to lose, and they don't have to be
colorful to get what they want anymore.
In our neighborhood, see the eternity of brick and stucco,
yellow, white, and brown, the tasteful flowers
that only shout, "I am rich."
In other places, violets lift their delicate heads,
but they sink back down,
they kneel in the humility of crumbling.
The passionflower diets on broken glass,
the morning glory cringes and clings to a pole,
and everything turns the color of these unpainted houses.
How we yield to a grayness,

to a scene almost without contrast,
to the macadam and the sky and the purple berries
that cluster at the tips of memory.
It is all there, the next day, and this one,
morning and fog and the rows of unpainted houses.
"The poor," I used to say, "who have nothing
but each other," as though words would redeem them
or their houses might be painted brighter
with kinder brushes than fire, as though every coat
would not soak in deeper, every color become this color —
color of the hawk's breast, color of absence.
And I go down Russell Street
where luxury is all a dissolution and the unpainted houses
are leaving one by one, like teeth,
like hair, like brittle sticks.
In their last seasoning, they sway and creak
this way and that,
in the wind's whole moment,
with their doors numberless, awaiting their condemnation.

TWO GIRLS AT THE
HARTSELLE, ALABAMA,
MUNICIPAL SWIMMING POOL

Too much of the country in their walk —
as though each struggled
against a tree at the center of her body,
or all the bare feet were shoes

that didn't fit, poverty in every step,
in every move, deliberate
as footsteps in plowed fields,
through clots of local boys, up

slippery rungs to the high board,
their bodies oiled, flipping away
casually the menthol cigarettes,
tossing back their bleached hair,

both twelve or thirteen years old:
like old houses, like mothers
pitched forward into the wind,
entering the cold, strange waters.

ALMA

SOMETIMES in late summer I come to
the husks of cicadas. In death
they are rooted in the scaly bark
of the pine,
become their own coffins,
these hard and glossy shells
that had contained
the secrets of flight.

That's why I like it in the South.
The afterlife is with you
all the time. It holds you
like that shack you pass
on the interstate,
so colorless and shapeless,
like all the rest of the world
you will never recognize
until it falls on you.

If I had learned in a better school
that offered more
than the lilyish English of Jesus,
I might have known, when I went to look up the word
that meant soul in my love's language,
that it would be Alma,
who cursed her picksack up the row ahead of me,
her black hair tied up with a red handkerchief,
her painted mouth opening,
and the black words loosening like crows.

In the fields, in the fifties, in Alabama,
there were women who loved to cha-cha,
bending all day to ruin their fingernails,

dragging behind them
the dead weight of cotton.
Full of work, their bodies were shaking
to the tinny beat of portable radios,
and their husbands were thinking
of joining the Church of God.

She died absurdly
at one of the sideshows
at the Limestone County Fair. Her heart
is no secret now, fabric
of a dimestore purse.

While most of the wives cowered
around booths of otherworldly vegetables,
while most of the husbands
were creeping down the midway to the girlie shows,
pausing to become the shadows of tents,
she listened to the trick-rider
gun the engine of his chrome Harley,
watched him spin up the impossible wall
of a giant barrel. Against
that din and blur, death must have seemed
a precipitate absentmindedness,
a freakish loss of balance.

I have always believed in the soul
that is lighter than the body's shadow
and the shadow
that drags a heavy sack
or pushes a plow oiled with dew.
I stand in my father's field
where Alma sang with the rich women
on the radio
of cheating hearts and ricochet romances.
Then I hear again the slow
engines starting in the pines,
the sharp and persistent voices
of cicadas.

RECURRENCE OF ACROPHOBIA AT AN ABANDONED QUARRY

ONCE when we climbed the limestone bluff
and all my friends had thrown themselves
into the tense air over the quarry,
I only stood at the edge, knowing that water
was a door that would never open for me.
Though every face surfaced, laughing,
I stepped back and knelt in the bramble,
the old fear rocking me like a colicky child.

From that summer, I can show the scars
made by adrenaline, the patient fluttering
of the heart flirting with a depth
it neither understood nor wanted.
I remember girls who would "go all the way,"
but one button at a time, into matrimony,
how their phone numbers festered just before sleep.
Sundays I carried my whole body up the face
of the bluff like the unsure hand of a lover.

Now they have siphoned all the water
from that hole where Jimmy Ponder drowned.
Alone this time, I struggle up the jut
to look down on the impenetrable bodies of boulders
going down in the all-hospitable earth.
Quarry dust fills the air. I whirl
to grab the scrub pine, feeling the fish-barb
bob and jerk at the center of appetite.

Twice this year in dreams I've plummeted
for hours into that hole which in life

I've only stood above, teasing the loss of nerve.
Twice, with her unimagining hand, my wife
has touched my brow, though that comfort
now is faint, and love was first imagined,
through a radio that played beside me here,
a good forty feet above the swimmers,
as an "endless falling," as a "walking on air."

AFTER THE MAQUILISUAT TREE

In San Salvador, where I died and was resurrected by sulfa,
        where I retched up my spirit
and heaved my soul, choked and heaved until the last distilled
        vinegar of green mango
was all there was clinging between me and the black dust of
        Bocaron,
I was not taken for William Walker, the conqueror, nor for
        Neruda, my hero, nor Cardenal;
but as myself, with a gringo's pinstripes and easily ruffled
        stomach,
I went around addled and lost, stupid for the unproffered
        sympathy.
And even before the airstrip at Ilopango, before the first
        soldiers with machine guns
and the firecrackers of the Salvadorean Christmas, I was too
        literal.
I was blinded by richness and fear as, later, I was rattled by
        traffic, moving
like a premonition among ambulances, my eyes going up to
        the dark holes between torches
or scurrying through doors with the scruffy goats and
        undernourished pigs.
At every stop, a ragamuffin battalion from the nearest barrio
hurled itself out of the shadows and flung itself across our
        windshield
as young women walked past us, balancing their impossible
        baskets, old women
humpbacked under bundles of firewood, and everywhere in the
        afternoon
the voices, the smoke, the sour and ubiquitous odor of wood
        and pupusas.

That first week, before the maquilisuat entered me and made
        me holy,

after the lemon slices of Spanish, the vodkas on breezy terraces,
where could I lie down and not think of the insects, of the
    poor filing like ants
up Bocaron to the fincas, and their champas that were
    mudwalled and patched with cardboard
and cellular like the nests of dirt daubers? In Alabama, they
    hover a few dusty weeks
of forever, neither larvae nor adults, their legs tucked up tight
into their blue bodies, their transparent wings too fragile to lift
    them.
But this was the dark gray and fecund dust of the volcano, a
    veil so immense
and impenetrable, a sudden hand, a flash of white shirt,
    glimpsed through the rifts torn
by small gusts, coagulated with the hotel palms, the opalescent
    waters.
In confusion, where conviction is strongest, I shuddered and
    reeled for three
slow days, the world spinning and gagging in the stomach's
    singular eye.

After the maquilisuat I gave up my pretensions to the earthly
    life:
my old French automobile, grinding in its lower gears,
and both my rugs, the one woven in India and the American
    one bordered
with blue flowers. I gave up my twelve hundred books, my last
    nine hundred
and seventy-three dollars. I would become Saint Dominicus,
for the bugs had tunneled into my body and mined the ore of
    my bowels.
The part of me trembling and whistling for martyrdom and the
    part of me aching for red meat
compromised on the melon, Thomas Jefferson, and the later
    poems of Rimbaud.
I ate slowly, one fat tortilla at a time, picking at the secret
    gristle of rat threading the butifarras.
Then from the lovely, the nearly leafless tree of summer,

from the pink gown of the eternal bridesmaid, I stripped away
    the millions of blossoms
to hold the smooth trunk, the naked limbs of that country in
    my arms.

In Alabama, where I come from, we are taken with the dark
    eyes of women, with the first spring
blossoms of dogwoods, redbuds, plums, peaches, apples, pears,
    and acacias.
In our longing, the world lays out its net, and we are caught
in the red dust the dirt dauber works in its mandibles, making
    a home.
In the old beauty we are caught, in the destruction, in the
    sickness and desire,
coughing into our handkerchiefs, dropping our forks into
    crevices,
shriveling and wrinkling like pears. One afternoon, south of
    winter,
when the snow was clumping on curbs in Minneapolis and
    lifting my country,
I snorkeled with my friends in a shallow pool dynamited from
    a cliff above the Pacific,
kicking my flippers and searching in the clear water for the
    little purple
and tiger-striped fish who are the shy and ever-wavering spirits
    of guilt.
What is that to me? To love a country, we must be composed
    of its dust,
take one tree into our bodies and, covered by pollen, bathe in
    its waters.

SIMULATED WOODGRAIN VINYL

I WAS not there long, between the housing project and the
    seediest of developments, the identical two-bedroom
brick or clapboard bungalows, advertised for newlyweds,
    occupied by the very old.
The house where I lived (mildewed and leaky, crosshatched
    with ancient wiring, its plaster and lath walls
still spindling and spider-cracking under the landlord's creamy
    K mart paneling) I shared
with a teenage mother who beat her child, and two fiftyish
    spinster sisters who every afternoon
walked their primped poodle past my front window down the
    street to the park.
Most days were artless, innocuous — rife with bad salesmen
    and fake catastrophes.
Nights the potboilers I took to bed revealed their feeble plots
    like pretty girls feigning bashfulness,
while the crescendo of Black Sabbath ravaged the Mormon
    Tabernacle Choir.

                Nothing else!
No ora, no aes, no smee, no Eris, no eider from the smalltown
    crossword puzzle!
I did not imagine my fate as the common one — infinitely
    distributable, statistical — stroking itself, clumsily, in the
    dark.
Neither did I conjure a forest from the unconvincing grain of
    those walls: trees with plastic leaves,
like the leaves that hem in coffins but do not diminish the
    immaculate corpse; and noble savages,
Tennessee Watusis popping their clutches in the parking lots of
    burger palaces.
But my thoughts were like those walls, like the side panels of
    stationwagons, like the basements of churches

where Little League coaches bully aphorisms from the chubby
sons of realtors.

There still must be some trinket, in a box I no longer unpack,
and obsolete keys, O necklace of lost addresses.
I've lived since then in twenty places, better and worse, that
run together now in the glaze
of abstract memory, totem of the vacant gaze, so all I have for
touchstone is one infantile, sugary tune,
one of the hits of that year, that still clings in what remote
precinct of the brain.
So the sauce the sisters stewed all day comes back with its
sickening garlic,
and the child who would not stop crying turns to me his
white, lopsided face, the way
a wave plants in darkened sand the treble hooks of a single
phosphorescent lure.

And what can I expect now? The whole boring ambience
swelling until I die of too much past,
die of the unassuaged guilts, the cumulative sighs, grunts, and
titters of disgust?
It's time to rearrange the stories, to milk permanence from the
walls.
These nights the moon's slow plow still opens its gash in the
sterile heavens above the Second Methodist Church.
Down the street, if my old house crumbles, most things
weren't meant to last, but do.
In memory, which admonishes loss and shines most repeating
the commonplace, even the paneling
takes on the shabby character of small airports and out-of-the-
way diners,
and I remember the older sister, how fiercely she held the
jeweled leash as she walked
toward her frog pond and magnolias, towing her twelve
pounds of affection.

DECADENCE

In the junque store the idlers were talking about primitives,
how scarred wood can be steeped in dignity, how that subtle
     patina
derives from hands, hands of the old, hands of the poor.
                    The hands of the dealer
were on the halltree, the cream separator, the set of burled
chestnut tools, as he whispered, *Williamsburg, Jamestown,*
     Monticello.
He was selling an incarnation of this country, not mere
     furniture,
patched and splaying relics, like that pie safe, still hopeful
                in its ugliness,
hewn crudely with a broadax, planed with bad iron for
     temporary uses.
I could remember how, in my grandmother's attic, dirt daubers
would construct their nests along the pegs
of an unworkable loom, and how one residential cell at a time
                would crumble,
dusting the human heirlooms stacked in boxes underneath:
delicate Japanese fans, mother-of-pearl combs, letters
from flung hamlets named for springs, groves, and crossroads.
Under the spectacles that I had found in a stray boot
                a bleached calligraphy
yielded its covered-dish suppers, its gaggle of Sunday
     visitations,
while time's odor, dull and implacable,
           stirred from a sidesaddle hooked on a rafter —
redolence of an old horse as he is being led from his last
     pasture.
Later, when the house was sold, the decadence broke out:

moths flopped sleepily out of giant black trunks,
and spiders, those shrewd solicitors of corners, invaded
with light that leaked fatally through shingle cracks,
gnawing the tablecloths, flawing the spokes of spinning wheels.
                              In the junque store
I could imagine the rage and falling away, the terrible ordeal
of finishing and refinishing, the worship of smooth surfaces,
and the patient preservation of flaws. I could love things
for hands that touched them, before grace, setting the plain
        tables.

                              2

In America there are many sacred places: improbable shrines,
                              Jerusalems of bed sheets,
dim synagogues where the spirit loiters, or sleeps, obsolescent
                              as that brakeman
I saw long ago on the L & N, waving his handkerchief from a
        caboose.
And here on my front porch, midnight, in Jefferson's paved
        Virginia,
all the good students are smoking dope and talking about God.
I watch them hesitate and plunge into history. They pass
the joint and I hear, in each voice, the blurred, icy dithyrambs
                              of Morpheus.
In each face I watch the moon that rises out of childhood,
                              largest light
against these small heavens resonating through
                              the wishful dark.
Here are our cosmic rose, our jockey of telepathy, our shaman
                              of the dimestore mantra.
The joint shrinks, passing from one to another, O orbital
        communion.

When the spirit moves you, don't be ascared, spake!
        Summer revival, 1958, Church of God,

I was watching, Mrs. Morgan
        was coming up like something partially
                        digested,
Mrs. Morgan was home from the nuthouse and she was
        coming
out of her pew like hot shrapnel of bad corn blasting the
        throat:
                        O Savior . . . hare me, Lord!
I have in me the creak of the wheelchair
        after the unsuccessful
                        laying on of hands,
the horror and beauty of it. I have belief rotting and going
bad in the stomach, old egg taste that comes to me like
        postcards
from places I'd rather forget. On the porch at midnight
                        the students
will grow silent. They will listen for the wind, the sweet
        summer evening,
a few stars diminishing slowly, darkening like the notes of a
        lullaby.

                                3

Once everyone was a Hemingway at the party where the girl
who painted penises stepped out of her clothes. Her pathetic
                        gosling neck of a body
clovered with goose bumps, and Christ! the luminous bad taste
                        of her art. I mean
banana penises rising from baskets of assorted fruits,
                        wienerwurst penises curled
in Dutch ovens, senile penises slumped in waterlogged dorics,
                        symbolic dorks and phalluses
of men we knew. I mean the night she painted
        her whole body purple
                        and crawled into a party
dragging two bowling balls, bobbing a prick-head of
        papier-mâché.

Now she teaches at the Y,
drives back and forth from the suburbs in the old
    stationwagon.
I love her, but it is not the same between us, her thighs
                like ponds silting
from underneath and glazing over, blue-green with varicose
    algae.
O aging mermaid of the suburbs, I shall teach you Prufrock
              in Continuing Ed,
and I promise not to embarrass you, to touch you lightly
as the monarch comes to the leaf of the black locust
or the wand of the Channel 4 weatherman touches a distant
    storm.
These nights I think you sleep as the wilderness sleeps beyond
    your windows,
                  anaesthetized,
while the city's nimbus dilates, strewing light
    by the ruined creeks.
              See how the stag
deer leaps and hesitates and is frozen in the headlights,
    the muskrat tunnels into a covert,
the rabbit works a pink sock into her nest of lespedeza and
    sedge.
No wonder the undertaker plays the harmonica! No wonder
there are psychiatrists everywhere ashamed of their singing!
    No wonder it is always Wednesday.

4

Old hands crusted over with eczema, otherworldly, cold
              and blunt as potatoes
on the back of the pew Wednesday nights, where we would go
    to pray,
and all the widows were hungry for God, like debutantes
             at the end of a boyless summer,

or nun-poets of the Dark Ages singing the sensual body of the
     church.
My grandmother, Mrs. Lyle, Mrs. Patterson, Viola Wilkins,
     Mavis Kent,
and a few others who could still pray, weep, and sing
     unabashedly,
each went down. Each languished in Bobby Summerford's
     rest home
                              in the perversity
of extravagant leisure — game hour, story hour.
     Near their deaths
                              not one of them believed
any man had walked on the moon. I am not concerned that
     they rot
sealed away from us, distant as the death of grocery chickens.
On the news there is a fly-bait hand, extending
     from the rubble.
                              I know, a man's hand,
hand of a believer in Allah. Some nights I dream that I am
     lost,
wandering among numberless houses, dangling like a root in a
     sewer.
One of my hands is rotting; I keep it in my shirt like
     Napoleon's hand.
This is that season, decadence in the leaf we look at. We sing
                              for the safe eggs,
sing with the iced fish in the Piggly Wiggly, the worms, the
     pale grass,
and the moon seems, yes, to sing, and the water sings in the
     spigot.
The old furniture sings mildew and mold, and I am happy
with my friends who remember a few jokes and are serious
                              at other times,
and with my friends who are at once joking and serious,
and with the most serious jokes, the music of Mozart and
     Brahms.

I think of the mayfly, who in adulthood forms perfect genitalia
                    but no stomach,
who lives for a single day to fly up and lay her eggs in the
        branches
of one of those willows that grow on small islands
        in the Tennessee River,
and I think of the fishermen, close by when the smallmouth
        gather
to wait for the end of the flight, when the exhausted come
        home.

Acknowledgments

These poems first appeared in the following magazines:

The Atlantic: "Baby Angels," "For the Eating of Swine," "The Mosquito"

Ironwood: "The Safety Lecture"

New England Review and Bread Loaf Quarterly: "The First Birth," "I Find Joy in the Cemetery Trees"

The New Virginia Review: "Fledglings"

Poetry: "For Those Who Miss the Important Parts," "Meditation on Birney Mountain"

The Poetry Miscellany: "The Magic Cloak," "Recurrence of Acrophobia at an Abandoned Quarry," "Sweep"

Poetry Northwest: "A Distant Weather," "A Hill of Chestnuts," "A History of Speech," "Alma," "Remembering Fire," "Some Futures," "Unpainted Houses"

River Styx: "After the Maquilisuat Tree," "Dirt," "Edisonesque," "Imagination," "The Man Who Thinks of Stallions"

Southern Humanities Review: "Responsibilities"

Swallow's Tale: "Curiosity," "Decadence," "Friends of the Poor," "The Laundromat at the Bay Station"

Virginia Quarterly Review: "Dry Socket," "Thoreau"

"A History of Speech" was reprinted in *The Pushcart Prize: IX*. "The First Birth," "For the Eating of Swine," "The Mosquito," "Remembering Fire," and "Thoreau" were reprinted in *The Morrow Anthology of Younger American Poets*.